Celebrate Recession with a Bottle of Champagne!

An Effective Guide on How to Earn while Businesses are Falling

By: Marc Foster

9781681279435

I0402555

PUBLISHERS NOTES

Disclaimer – Speedy Publishing LLC

This book was originally printed before 2014. This is an adapted reprint by Speedy Publishing LLC with newly updated content designed to help readers with much more accurate and timely information and data.

Speedy Publishing LLC

40 E Main Street, Newark, Delaware, 19711

Contact Us: 1-888-248-4521

Website: http://www.speedypublishing.co

REPRINTED Paperback Edition: 9781681279435:

Manufactured in the United States of America

DEDICATION

This book is dedicated to Barbara, the only woman I have ever felt this way with.

TABLE OF CONTENTS

Chapter 1- The Recession-Induced Wealth Craze 5

Chapter 2- How to Get Rich in a Recession Gold Rush..................... 9

Chapter 3- Triple Your Money When Everyone Else is Losing...14

Chapter 4- Secret Tips to Surviving Tough Economic Times......18

Chapter 5- Pay Up while Interest Rates are Down 32

Chapter 6 – Protect Your Income 35

Chapter 7 – Best Legal Strategies to Keep Businesses from Closing 41

Chapter 8 – Accept the Possibility of a Move 44

About The Author... 48

CHAPTER 1 - THE RECESSION-INDUCED WEALTH CRAZE

When the economy is in a recession, expect that there would be a race for all persons who want to become rich even if the economic condition is not good. This aim is possible for everyone and if you are aiming for this, you have to believe that there is a great chance for you to do so. You can do it if you know what you need to do so that you will win in the race. Recession races happen around the world today and there are people who get rich and win in these races.

Becoming rich during a recession appears to be an oxymoron. You have to keep in mind that credit is rigid when there is a recession. There are fewer jobs to offer and if people will try to become rich during this situation, they will strive for it against each other. This is how the race will start.

If you want to join the race and become the winner, there are certain things that you can do to get more chances to make the economic recession a great opportunity for you to prosper. There is no need to change the usual way you live. Instead, you have to rise up and be brave to face the impact of the challenging economy.

If you see that it is applicable, you can try to become more productive in your present job. You may ask for overtime to raise additional income. Make the management of the company where you work impressed with your work ethic and your ability to examine the details. Second, you have to assess your budget and refrain from spending your money on unimportant things so that you can save money. Always remember that spending less and being wise in buying are helpful to anyone who wishes to prosper even while the economy declines.

Also, you may opt to change your driving habits. You can sell your low gasoline mileage car and replace it with a more efficient one or you can even choose a public vehicle. Always maintain the car to improve its efficiency and to lessen your repair expenses. If you are planning to go back to school, you may look for financial assistance options available. These offerings will let you pay the expenditure after you graduate.

You may also sell all your unwanted items in your garage. Offer a garage sale or you may use the auction websites or online classified ads to liquidate the excess and to pay your debt at the same time. During an economic recession, people tend to look for the items they need at cheaper costs.

Also, you should monitor the bond and stock markets from time to time. Markets usually fluctuate more throughout a recession. To win the race, you need to be updated with the statistics for unemployment rates.

Financial races happen every time a recession affects the economy of a country. There is nothing wrong if you aim for riches even if the economy's condition is not good. To win, you have to do the steps mentioned above. With your strong determination to achieve success, winning in the recession race will not be hard for you to attain.

What is the Modern-Day Gold Rush?

If the global economy is under the influence of full-fledged recession, what usually happens together with the economic turbulence is the modern-day gold rush. As the experts were able to say yes and express their acceptance of the fact, most of them stressed the advantage of gold investment throughout the times when the economy is under depression or recession.

The reason they want to emphasize gold investment is that it will keep them updated with the actual prices of gold in the market. The commodity has had inverse correlations together with the world's economy.

Primarily, if the economy is in a down situation, gold will strive and will attempt to reach and create a record of high prices. All cash is backed up by gold and thus this commodity will be the safest investment in the market.

On the other hand, as the opposite relationship between the world economy and gold is a powerful and a historically precise trend, nothing is a hundred percent sure particularly with investing. The best thing to do is to start investing your money in gold and in the other metals. However, you have to make sure that you have a consistent connection to the coin brokers, dealers and other firms concerned with gold investment. This way, you will get an idea about the actual price of gold.

Celebrate Recession with a Bottle of Champagne!
Although gold is substantially more stable compared to any other commodity where you can invest your money, you should never stay too calm and believe that everything is fine. Always find out the recent price and the value of this commodity to ensure that all your investments are secured and safe. This will also enable you to track all your earnings to know where your money goes. Gold investment is not an investment that is typically included in the advertisements, but this is also a sound investment that you could make.

Purchasing gold when the economy is under recession is already a traditional strategy. During the year 1930, 1970s and 1980s when depression affected the economy, people went altogether to buy gold or silver and treated them as a safe haven. People who buy gold usually extend themselves too much for investing to stave off the decline of the economy.

Although the situations are not severe in the same way as the present scenario, the basic rule remains similar. People tend to abandon their investments for other commodities and they choose gold so that they can keep their funds. This will let them make money to get the amount they have invested. In the present economic landscape, this metal is among the investments that could help their financial health.

CHAPTER 2- HOW TO GET RICH IN A RECESSION GOLD RUSH

You know that gold is often among the best options when it comes to investment. The first among the gold rushes in the world revealed the fact that there are more people who are really eager to become rich. These people are those who are too much interested in this shiny and precious metal.

Way back before, gold was considered as one of those things that serve as the basis of the wealth of a person. Nowadays, this metal is accessible to all investors whether they are rich or average. It is obvious as even the countries with a smaller population are the major investors for gold. The main reason behind this is that this metal may go up higher in the succeeding years. Compared to any other investments, gold has a good value which can't be overlooked.

Gold has been one of the most appreciated assets for several decades. Though investing in real estate used to be considered the best option, the present economic crisis and recession which conquered the whole world showed that it is not the best choice for investors at all.

Most of the investors who prefer to invest in real estate properties lose their money as it influenced the success of most creditors and most especially, those banks that are known to be the most firm ones around the world.

The question that you might have right now is "how do investors get more money if they invest in gold?" Becoming rich in a recession gold rush will be possible if you do the following:

1. Find out the actual cost of gold in the market today. Always keep in your mind that it will increase every day. If you will compare the cost of it with its previous costs before, you will see that it is higher than before. Some investors speculate that people expect a market bubble to happen. Therefore, you have to hurry up and buy gold while you still have the chance to do so. In some years, the cost of this metal will go higher and this will provide more chance for all investors to earn money and become rich.

2. Gold is always in demand and things may change around you. It is the result of innovations and advancements in technology. It is not the case when it comes to this precious metal. This has been there for several years and it is always appreciated by millions of people around the world.

3. Those who want to invest in gold are the people who are really determined to become rich. Among the best means to prove this claim is by considering the way that the richest men and women of the world got all their money. These people invested their money in gold once and most of them preferred to keep on investing their money in gold.

These are just some of the reasons why most people became rich as they invested their money in this precious metal. So perhaps, gold is indispensable in most industries. This might be the right time for you to make an investment and choose gold. What you need to do is to begin purchasing small coins or bars of gold.

The 5 Mistakes You Should Not Commit

Recession always results in a race and winning on it will lead to a better life. To survive and beat all hurdles to achieve success, you know that there are certain things that you need to do to attain your goal. However, taking precautionary measures and knowing what you should never do when there is a recession is also important. The following are the five things you should never do so that you can win the race:

• Cosigning a loan – doing this is just like putting yourself deeper in the hole of economic deficit. In the event that the borrower of the money fails to pay his or her debt, you will be the one to pay that. When the economic condition is not good, the risks related to loan cosigning can be even more because it might become a reason for you to lose your job so both you and the borrower will not be able to make payments at all.

• Obtaining an adjustable rate mortgage – when buying a home, there are some people who choose the adjustable-rate mortgage or ARM. In some instances, this action might be advantageous.

As the amount of interest is low, the amount to be paid per month would be low at the same time. On the other hand, what if you lose your job and the interest rate of the mortgage went higher while the recession begins? While the rate increases, the charged amount you need to pay every month might also go up. In this situation, you may find that it is really difficult to look for money so that you can pay your obligation. Always bear in your mind that overdue payments and non-payment could have a huge impact on your own credit rating. This could prevent you from getting loans in the succeeding months.

- Taking on additional debt – asking for a new loan might not be an issue when you are capable enough to make payments for it. You can apply for it as long as you have a stable source of profit. On the other hand, what will happen if your source of living is affected by recession? What might happen to you if you lose your job? In most cases, unemployed individuals take the job opportunities with lower salary rates than their previous jobs just to sustain all their needs and to have money which they can use to pay their obligations. Unluckily, the amount to be earned is completely too far from the amount they earn from their previous jobs. When it happens to you, all your savings will be lost. So, if you are planning to get another loan today, think about it first and consider the possible consequences that may happen in case you lost your job. Taking new debts when there is an economic recession is full of risk and you have to be careful about this.

- Being careless in your job – during a recession, you have to realize that the companies, particularly the larger ones might be under the influence of financial pressure. When it happens, most companies will try to lessen their expenditures as much as possible. In other cases, they may result to scaling back to the operations of the company, like holiday parties. Sometimes, companies prefer to cut the bonuses they pay and the worse is that they are forced to terminate other employees so that the company can survive without having too many expenses. This is one of the strategies of the companies today as they know that having more employees will bring more expenses for them. As the employment status throughout the recession might be extremely sensitive, employees like you should do everything that you can to ensure that your employer will consider you as among the most valuable employees of his or her company. You can do this by coming to work early, spending more hours working and performing all responsibilities properly. As there is no guarantee that it could save you, it will be the qualities that your employer will appreciate from you.

- Taking risks while making investments – the owners of business are always thinking about their business and its future. They tend to look for ways to make their business grow. On the other hand, recession might not be the right time to invest. A good example of this is taking a loan to provide an additional space for products. What if your business fails to develop? Would you have money to pay the loan on time? When it comes to investment, you should be careful and you need to consider the probable consequences that you may experience when this situation happens.

CHAPTER 3- TRIPLE YOUR MONEY WHEN EVERYONE ELSE IS LOSING

Recession is a race and everyone is aiming to be the winner. To make sure that you will be able to achieve your objective, you need to make sure that you are the "killer winner" in the race. Here are 7 tips that you can follow to be sure to win the recession race:

1. Concentrate on opportunities and make contributions.

2. Look for the most effective means to make yourself be more productive in your job. Try to do more things in less span of time. Whenever you go to work, always make sure that you will be able to finish everything that you need to do for that day.

3. Make your own self be more valuable and you can do it by learning more through education. It might be the right time for you to enroll in an MBA program or study in a law school. These are good options for you, especially if this is your dream. Financial assistance programs for education are always available and you can apply for these whenever you need to.

4. Stay positive and ignore those people who think negatively. Always believe that your own destiny is different and there is something good that waits for you in the future. The influence of the people around you matters but they are actually not necessary.

5. Develop the core of your strengths. When you find that it is hard to look for a good job within the marketing management industry, you may proceed to other related fields such as salesperson most especially if you are good in this.

6. Always keep in mind that some people will grow and achieve success while others will remain in the same way they were before. During a recession, you will see some people who are savvy and hardworking and they can do more compared to others as they believe that they can do everything to save their jobs.

7. Everything happens for a reason and the economy is not an exemption to this rule. Sooner, recessions will happen but this will not be permanent. All you need to do is to make sure that you are prepared to face this economic situation.

During the times when recession conquers the economy, people tend to concentrate more on retreating and cutting losses. Instead of this, you should focus on dealing with it, beating and making sure that you will win.

Celebrate Recession with a Bottle of Champagne!
Fatten Your Bank Account

Economic recession might be a scary situation but there are ways to face and overcome it. The first thing that you can do to fight recession is to do everything that can to earn more income. The main thing here is to take advantage of this situation and do everything you can instead of allowing yourself to be the victim. In fact, there are ways to make more cash even when the economy's condition is not good. Here are the steps you need to follow to make it possible:

• Odd jobs and look for online and home-based jobs. These are among the best means to earn additional income. Everything you do where you can get additional income would help you a lot in overcoming recession. Inside the economy where all people are looking for the ways to save money, it will be better if you will use your skill to make goods or offer services that can help other people. When it comes to recession, offering peculiar job opportunities to your friends, neighbors or family could be a great way to make and earn extra income. Expenditures are inevitable even when the economy is under recession. When you have spare time after work, you may look for the freelance jobs available on the web. These opportunities will let you make more money, which could be more than your regular salary.

There is a fact that some people are forced to sell their personal items because of the lack of stable source of money. This is the outcome when people lose their jobs. There are several people who are willing to vend their personal things like gadgets at cheaper prices for the sake of their urgent need for money that is triggered by recession. If you have some spare cash and you want something to buy, this could be the right time for you to do so especially if you know that somebody is selling the item you want. However, buying items which you do not really need yet would not be helpful if you feel the effect of recession. You should bear in your mind that you need to make more money and spend less of it.

- In recession, working extended hours might not be the best choice for everyone. For those people who are willing to do it, they will be able to make some additional money that they can add to their savings in the long run. When you are recently employed and you get nothing for your overtime, then it is not the option for you. It would be better if you will look for the career opportunities that will let you make and earn income. Making an effective financial plan is among the strategies to make more money even when there is an economic recession. Just be sure that you are aware of the ways that will really generate income so that you can focus more on attaining your goal.

CHAPTER 4- SECRET TIPS TO SURVIVING TOUGH ECONOMIC TIMES

Economic recession might be a usual aspect of the economy but it doesn't mean that dealing with this can be done easily. There are more people who suffer from this in some countries around the world.

As there are more problems associated with the industry of real estate economy and there are more people who lose their jobs, people start to worry about the possible things that may happen in their lives. When you have a good and stable job, recession will not be a big problem in your case but it doesn't mean that you just have to relax and do nothing about it.

When there is an economic recession, people might be affected in different ways. The way you will survive from this will depend on the way you deal with it. Here are the things that you can do to make sure that you will be a winner in the recession race:

- **Understand Recession**

1. Be aware about recession and the possibility of when it may affect the economy of the country where you live. Listen to the news and be watchful of all events related to economy. By knowing the details about recession, you will be able to make a plan on how you will deal with this.

2. Make your loved ones understand recession and ask them to help you. Dealing with the recession in the economy and ensuring that you and your loved ones will be able to survive is a responsibility of each member of your family. Your son and daughter could also help you by ensuring that they avoid wasting the food served on the table and that they are wise in using water and electricity. These will help you a lot in reducing the monthly expenditures of your family for the utility bills and food consumption. When the light is not in use, ask them to turn it off whenever they have to leave. Always remind your kids to turn off the television if they are not interested in the show at all. By doing these simple things, you will be able to save some money.

3. Ask your neighbors and encourage them to help you. When the economy is under the influence of recession, it means that all people who live in the affected country will suffer from the effects of this. Teach your neighbors about the things you know that will help in overcoming the negative impacts of recession.

- **Put Some Money Away**

Keep saving easy by taking yourself out of the equation. Utilize your bank's auto-draft feature to schedule steady transfers from your checking account to your savings account. Then, take it easy; and let the bank manage all of the particulars for you.

Celebrate Recession with a Bottle of Champagne!

Did you get a raise at work? Try not to consider it as an opportunity to super-size your life-style, but a chance to super-size your savings. Step-up your 401(k) savings by the sum of your raise, or use your auto-draft to put the extra money in savings. Then, continue on with your current lifestyle. Accessible income is money that's likely to get spent up.

Keep your savings unreachable by sticking it at a different bank than your checking account. The additional hassle of going to another bank will make you think twice about using it. CDs and savings bonds are likewise good savings tools for keeping money out of view.

Saving change is in no way a fresh idea, but there's a reason for that: it actually works. Make a habit of putting all of your change into a jar each night. Then, put the money into a savings account when the jar is full. To hike up your savings even more, make a game out of searching for coins in parking areas. It's even more amusing to save, when you're saving somebody else's money.

Do you take part in a lot of rebate offers? If so, think about sticking all of your rebate checks into a savings account. You aren't in all likelihood going to miss the money, but you're likely to like getting those savings statements in the mail. Illness, job loss, house repairs, auto repairs--there are so many matters that may rock your financial ship.

Are you organized to address them? Begin an emergency fund, and you won't have to question. Determine how much you'd like to put away. A thousand, 3 to 6 month's living expenses, a year's wages. There many opinions out there about how much income you should place into an emergency fund, but the only view that matters is yours. Ask yourself how much you'd need to have put away to feel safe, and make that the amount that you lay aside in your emergency fund.

Establish a list of all of your steady monthly expenses, housing costs, food, utilities, debt repayments, transit costs, insurance and all of your other "must-pay" bills. Then, total your month-to-month expenses, and multiply the resulting figure by the number of month's that you decided to put away. For instance, if you need to cover $2,500 in every month expenses for 3 months, you'll need to allow for $7,500 in your emergency fund.

Once you've ascertained how much you need to save, it's time to choose where you'll keep your money. Because you want your emergency fund to stay fairly accessible, a savings account, money market account or short-run CD make common sense. Any one of these accounts will provide you the liquidness that you need, while still bringing in some interest. If you're like most individuals, it's going to take time to develop your emergency fund, likely even a lot of time. That's all right. The crucial thing is that you get moving now.

Look over your finances, and ascertain how much you are able to afford to put toward your emergency fund monthly. Even a little will help, so don't worry if that's all you are able to afford to do.

Turn a creative eye on your finances, and you're sure to discover ways to reach your savings goal quicker.

- **Stop Wasting Money**

Postpone or do away with unneeded purchases. Then, add the savings to your emergency fund.

Celebrate Recession with a Bottle of Champagne!
Cutting down on your spending does not have to mean lots of giving up of things. Try out a few of these painless cost cutters, and observe your spending reduce to a more comfortable level.

Fancy Name brand products are great, but regular store brand products are frequently even as good (if not one in the same). Make the change over to the bargain labels, and you will shave twenty-five to fifty percent off of your weekly grocery store bill. With increasingly more grocery store chains bringing out their own line of organics and additional premium products, there's never been a more comfortable time to shift.

Have you ever gone to the store for a couple of particulars and emerged with a whole trunk full of things? Who hasn't? To prevent impulse shopping from grabbing your budget, make a habit of shopping with a list. Write down everything you need, and then merely shop for those items. You might be still enticed to add an extra item to your cart. Head home and consider it first. If you still need the item you are able to always add it to your next shopping list.

Dining out always costs more than dining at home — whether it's a speedy snack from a convenience store, a vending machine or a fast food place. Prevent this cost altogether by keeping snacks on hand at all times. Put a granola bar and a bottle of some sort of beverage in your purse or satchel before running errands; squirrel away some goodies in your desk drawer at work--just be prepared for that hunger attack where and if it decides to come up. Whether it's food in your pantry, hobby provisions or beauty care merchandise, you likely have lots of unused or partially utilized items around your home.

Before you dash out to the store to purchase your next "must-have," look around and see if you are able to find something at home to fill your requirement. This easy exercise won't only help you to spend to a lesser extent, but likewise to clean out some of the clutter in your house. Challenge yourself to save more every time you go out to shop. If you generally purchase something at regular price, challenge yourself to discover it on sale.

If you generally purchase something on sale, challenge yourself to discover it on clearance. When you're forever on the lookout for a deal, there's no end to the money that you are able to save; and before long it becomes a game that you look forward to acting on.

- **Stockpile**

Prices may be a bit irregular during a recession. The resolution? Establish a reserve of sale-priced foods and commodities, and you'll only have to purchase when it's a good deal for you. Stockpiling is a basic practice among frugal people and for good cause: it may save a ton. If you're sick of paying full price for your foodstuffs, it might be time to begin a stockpile of your own. Here's how it works:

- Assemble a list of all the items that you utilize on a steady basis (food and differently). Make sure to include toiletries, paper products, cleansers and pet provisions (if needed).

- List the particulars on your stockpile list in a notebook, and start tracking how much you pay for them. Take exceptional care to notice any sales that you chance upon, along with the date of the sale and the name of the store where you discovered it.

- After a couple of months, your price book will show a good deal of valuable info, including what you commonly pay for things, which store has the better price on each item on your list and even how often particular sales happen.

- A stockpile only saves money when it bears particulars that have been bought on sale or gotten free of charge, so don't anticipate that you'll construct a huge stockpile overnight. Center your efforts on discovering those too good-to-pass-up sales and the stockpile will take form on its own:

- Try to spot the sale leaders in the weekly sales circulars

- Clip coupons, and match them to sales

- Blend manufacturer coupons and store coupons to maximize your savings

- Capitalize on rebate offers

- Snap up clearance items

Stockpiling is easy to exaggerate. Before you go crazy and purchase eighty-nine tubes of toothpaste, spend some time measuring your actual needs. Some stockpilers purchase enough of a particular to get to the next sale, while other people want to purchase enough to get through a particular number of months.

Whichever technique you pick, it's crucial to keep expiration dates in mind. You won't save any money by purchasing more than you are able to use: As your stockpiling skills better, you're going to start to uncover more gratis and nearly-free deals.

A little of advice from a veteran stockpiler: only stockpile things that you'll really utilize. If your loved ones didn't eat a certain brand of cereal when you purchased it at full-price, they won't eat it when you get it free of charge either.

Once those deals start to amass, you'll need to discover a way to organize them.

1st step: assigning a spot in your house for your stockpile. Pantries and cellars are good — if you've got them — However guest room closets, empty drawers and even that space under your bed will work.

Think creatively, and you'll discover the perfect spot for your stockpile. Then, your only challenge will be maintaining your stockpile in a neat and orderly way.

A couple of ideas to get you going:

- Put like items together

- Revolve your stock, pushing fresh items to the back and moving aged items to the front

- Freeze flour before stashing away to avoid bug Infestations

- **Make Do with what's Available**

No need to purchase new when you are able to make do. Consume leftovers; discover substitutes for items that you've run out of; find new uses for the things that you already have; and you'll keep that shopping list withering month after month.

Has a great sale or harvest left you with more food than you are able to utilize now? No need to let it go to waste. Here are directions for freezing a few foods you might have never entertained freezing:

- Eggs

Combine the yolks and egg whites collectively, and pour into an ice cube tray. 2 cubes are equal to one large egg.

- Milk

Keep it in its original container, but take out enough milk to allow for expansion – around 1 cup per gallon of milk. Defrost in the refrigerator, and shake well prior to using.

- Butter

Keep it in its original container. Defrost in the refrigerator to utilize.

- Bananas

Freeze in the peel. Then, merely thaw and peel to utilize in smoothies and breads. Note: the peel will turn dark, but that won't affect the caliber of the banana in the least.

- Celery

Wash and cut to wanted size. Then, quick-freeze on a tray, and transfer to a freezer bag or a different airtight container. To utilize: add the frozen celery directly to soups or other hot dishes.

- Tomatoes

Wash well. Then, freeze whole and unpeeled on a tray. Put in freezer bags once totally frozen.

Marc Foster

- Fresh Herbs

Cut finely. Then, put in an ice cube tray along with a small bit of water. To utilize: merely drop frozen cubes directly into hot dishes.

- Nuts

Freeze (either in shell or shelled) in a deep-freeze bag or another airtight container.

- Zucchini and Other Squash

Wash and chop to wanted size. Then, blanch for 3 minutes; let cool; and freeze in an airtight container.

- Apples

Freeze whole or chopped up, peeled or unpeeled.

Vinegar can be utilized to clean your house, to make health and beauty products, to do away with pests and more. Vinegar makes stain removal a snap. Here are some ideas using white vinegar and a bit of effort.

- Tomato Stains

Saturate the stain with vinegar. Let it soak in. Then, launder.

- Sugar-Based Stains

Saturate the stain with vinegar. Let it soak in. Then, launder.

• Coffee/ Tea Stains

Flush the area with vinegar to withdraw the stain. Rinse off and repeat as required. Then, launder as usual.

• Wine Stains

Saturate the stain with vinegar, and let it stand for numerous minutes. Then, rinse off with water, and duplicate the process, if required. Launder right away after.

• Mustard Stains

Put vinegar on the stain, and let it soak in. Then, spot treat with a little laundry detergent, and launder.

• Grease

Soak the stain in pure white vinegar. Then, launder as usual.

• Sweat Stains

Pour vinegar over the sweat stain. Then rub coarse salt into the stain (common salt will work if it's all you have). Put the garment out in the sun to dry. Then, launder.

• Grass Stains

Put vinegar on the stain with a sponge, and gently dab to lift. If the stain remains, make a spread of vinegar and baking soda, and brush it into the stain with an old toothbrush. Then, launder as usual.

- Ink Stains

Apply vinegar to the stain. Then, rub with a spread made of vinegar and baking soda. Let dry. Then, launder.

- Deodorant Stains

Rub vinegar into the stain till it disappears. Then, launder as usual.

- **Make it good until the Last Drop**

Are you tired of buying new razor blades, printer cartridges and additional household necessities every so often? Here's how to make some of those items last longer:

- Shampoo and Conditioner

Store bottles inverted to keep the shampoo or conditioner from bogging down at the bottom of the bottle. When you can't get any more out, add a couple capfuls of water, and then shake.

- Toothpaste

Once you've forced out as much toothpaste as you are able to, cut the tube open with a scissors, and you'll have enough for a lot more brushings. Store the cut tube in a plastic bag between uses to avoid dry out.

- Razors

Dry the blades off following every use, and they'll remain sharp longer.

• Shower Gel

Put your shower gel on a loofah, rather than on your skin, and a little squirt will bring forth endless lather.

• Lipstick

When you arrive at the bottom of a tube, use a lip brush or a Q-tip to get to the left over lipstick. Put your lipstick leftovers into an empty lip gloss pot for easy on the go utilization.

• Bar Soap

Undo your soap and let it dry for a couple weeks before you use it. How come? This is because dry soap does not dissolve as quickly when it comes into contact with water.

• Laundry Detergent

More detergent does not mean fresher clothes; it just means more soap residual on your clothes. Try utilizing half as much detergent as the manufacturer advocates, and you probably won't even notice the difference.

• Spray Cleaners

Set the spray nozzle to the lowest mist setting. Less emerging means less being utilized.

• Clothing

What's an easy way to stretch the life of all your clothes? Omit the dryer. All that heat just is not good for your clothes.

• Shoes

Remove dirt and scuff marks off of your shoes as soon as you observe them to avoid any permanent harm.

• Food

Food spoilage is frequently the result of unsuitable storage. Learn how to store the foods that you eat on a regular basis.

• Candles

Put candles in the freezer for a few hours before you utilize them. This will cause the wax to burn slower and more equally.

• Mattresses

Follow the manufacturer's ideas for flipping and rotating your mattress to avoid premature sagging.

• Refrigerators

Vacuum the condenser coil every 3 months (once monthly if you have animals).

• Markers

Renovate dried out markers by stashing away vertically (tip down) for a day or two. If that does not work, try dipping the tips in alcohol for a couple of minutes.

Chapter 5- Pay Up while Interest Rates are Down

A recession is not all sorry news. Since rates of interest tend to go down during recessive periods, your debts will cost you less; and your debt repayment dollars will go farther. It's a good time to pay down charge card debt. Look over your budget, and ascertain if you are able to afford to use more money to pay off your debt. Likewise keep an eye on the mortgage rates. Now may be the time to refinance to a lower interest rate and a shorter mortgage term.

To pay off your debt, you need to:

1. Evaluate Your Debt

2. Produce a Budget

3. Cut down Your Spending

4. Begin Saving

5. Attack Your Debt

If you are ready to put your debts to rest once and for all and truly begin paying it down, Here are some ideas to bring in some extra cash to put toward your debt reduction efforts:

- You are able to have a garage sale. Extra debris around the house is income just waiting to be liquefied. Gather up all of your old clothes, playthings, house wares, and pieces of furniture, and have a garage sale. Then put the money you make toward your debt of choice. If you have valuable items to sell- think about listing them on EBay or in the classified section of your local paper.

- As we discussed before you are able to save your change. Do you have a change jar? If you don't have one then get one. If you do, it's time to get into it. Roll all of your coins, and then make an additional debt payment equal to the amount that you've rolled up. Duplicate the process every time your jar is full.

- You are able to use coupons. Using coupons is a good way to save money on the things that you require, however it may likewise be a great way to advance your debt repayment attempts. Challenge yourself to utilize as many coupons as you are able to when you grocery shop, and then repay your efforts by placing the money saved toward your debt.

- You are able to hire yourself. Do you employ somebody to cut your grass or clean your home? If so, it might be time to hire yourself for the task. Take on a couple of the tasks that you'd commonly hire somebody else to do, and then "pay yourself" by putting the savings towards your debt.

Celebrate Recession with a Bottle of Champagne!

- You are able to share your views. Do you have views? Turn them into a paycheck by signing on for paid online surveys. You are able to complete as many or as few as you've time for, and then put the money toward paying off a debt early.

- You are able to turn cash gifts into payments. Do you have a relative that likes to send you money as a gift? Then pass that gift on to one of your credit cards, and watch your account balance come down.

- You are able to cash in on a talent. Hobbies are commonly a source of spending, but that doesn't have to be the norm. Establish a list of all of the things that you're good at, and then brainstorm ways to turn them into a reservoir of revenue. Can you give knitting lessons? Hire yourself out as a painter? Become a part-time landscape gardener? Discover a way to promote your skill or skills, and then turn your earnings into payments.

- You are able to bank your bonuses. We all profit from the occasional bonanza, whether it's a work bonus, an income tax return or something else totally. Vow to turn your bonus income into bonus debt repayments, and wring your hands over those credit card statements a bit less.

CHAPTER 6 – PROTECT YOUR INCOME

If you work for or own a company that's going to feel very little issues as a result of a recession you've very little to worry about. Irrespective of what company you work for, all the same, now is a capital time to begin making yourself indispensable. It's simple fact that the employees that are the 1st to go when lay-offs happen are the ones who aren't viewed as crucial enough to stay.

Making yourself an indispensable part of your company is the opening move making sure you maintain your income. Even companies that are cutting back their staff are going to pause with persons who are crucial to their company's daily operations. If you are able to, involve yourself in many projects your company is working on (plainly without stretching yourself so thin that you're no longer able to do a good job). The more things you have your fingers in, the harder it will be to let you go.

In times of recession companies might be cutting down on their employees, but that doesn't mean that they're going to be able to cut down on the amount of work they have to do. It simply means that that work is going to be re-delegated. If you're already actively involved in a lot of projects the company will feel it much easier to give you extra duties on these projects than to try to bring a fresh man up to speed.

This isn't the time to try to apply for a promotion or a transfer. The moment you accept this type of move you get to be the new man on the totem pole, and directly become more vulnerable when the time arrives to go through and choose who will go and who will stay. Mental attitude counts.

When companies are attempting to decide who will stay and who will go, often mental attitude and the employee's ability to boost team spirit is as strong a determiner as their ability to do their job. Remember, companies attempting to stay on top during a recession are going to have greater expectations of their employees than ever before. The only way these employees are going to be able to fulfill those expectations is if they're able to keep their morale high.

Hopefully the economic recession isn't going to impact your income stream-but that doesn't mean you shouldn't take safeguards. It's all about networking. If you've remained in touch with your bosses and associates, both past and current, you'll not only likely already know who's hiring and who's not; you might have the inside track when it comes to finding another job. If you wait to connect with them till you've been laid off, however, you're going to discover yourself scrambling.

They're going to know that the only reason you're getting hold of them is because you're hoping to acquire a job, and they're going to view you unfavorably. Regardless how much you've been looking ahead to spending the next 3 weeks on vacation, when your company begins making budget cuts is utterly, positively not the time to take an long vacation. You can't show somebody how useful you are if you're not there! That doesn't mean you have to strip yourself of a well-earned workweek away from the office.

If you tend to take your vacations in mass (disappearing for 2 to 3 weeks at a time) this is a good opportunity to spread those vacations out a little. No one expects you to work yourself to your demise.

Have a Backup Plan

Produce another income stream, even a little one. Perhaps you take a second job for a month to pay off a credit card or perhaps you sell your baseball cards on EBay or perhaps you find another way to begin a small business on the side. As the economic system moves closer and closer to a worse situation, we've seen many layoffs happening. How do you protect yourself and make sure you have a little extra coming in?

Companies aren't hiring, have started process improvement efforts and are viewing ways to cut costs by delaying equipment and software upgrades. Getting laid off in a beneficial economy isn't as big of a deal as when the economy is in a recession. Occasionally it even pays to get off the ship before it sinks.

If you've a good chance of getting laid off in the next year, you may prefer to consider finding another job while you still have a job. That way, you are able to move to the next job with minimum income loss. The most beneficial way to avoid a layoff is to have your own clients.

The one thing that I disfavor the most about working for somebody else is that when you leave – they keep the clients. The clients are the gems of any company, furnishing the revenue to pay the expenses and the employees. When push comes to shove, employees are let go, but the owners keep the clients that the employees have worked hard to acquire.

Business owners don't get fired, although they may go bankrupt if they get too far in debt. I'm not advising you give up your day job and begin a business – at any rate not before you've done your homework.

Beginning a business takes a lot of work, patience, money and a rare amount of ambition. Most individuals only succeed after bombing several times. What I am advising is that you consider setting up the basis of a small side business.

You may begin your business as a hobby and slowly begin adding clients. If you get fired, you'd have the basis all setup and a small client base already in place. This gives you the choice of either returning to find a different job or centering on your small business for income. A small business may be your insurance – reducing your risk of a fiscal hardship.

Drastic changes in the economic system will push a lot of businesses into bankruptcy and fresh products and services will be needed that weren't needed a short time ago. For instance, the need for foreclosure info and counselors has skyrockets in just the last six months.

A lot of individuals will be seeking fresh ways to live with the changes all around them. If you're seeking business ideas, I'd look at the needs of a recession economy. Your most beneficial protection from a layoff is to get your own clients.

Marc Foster
Rethink Your Investment Strategy

Move your investments to lower-risk securities like bonds during the market shakedown, than move back to stocks after the market hits the bottom – in a couple of years. A different option is to invest in commodities like gold, silver, wheat and corn, which are bringing back high profits, but they're also very risks, so be heedful and don't bet the farm.

The drastic market conditions have taken quite a chunk out of many 401k balances this year. The biggest headache is that the dollar is replaced as the world's Reserve Currency with the Euro or Yen or several other currencies or combinations.

The dollar is seesawing on collapse as the world is draining of willingness to continue to lend money to us as the global financial crisis is reversing their investments in dollars. We may choose to brush aside the evidence against the dollar all we want, but sooner or later the evidence will demand a finding of fact.

Here are a few other reasons that the world may face a dollar currency crisis very soon.

In light of this economic assessment, we might want to move money out of the bond market prior to the dollar dropping anymore. Sure, bonds are dependable if you just want to conserve your dollars, but most of us don't want our dollars back after they have lost ninety percent of their worth.

I likewise think many of the foreign markets are over sold from the rush to the bond market with little regard for the company's earnings.

Celebrate Recession with a Bottle of Champagne!

When the dollar drops, rising prices will come back with a vengeance and that will drive up the prices of trade goods – particularly gold.

Stay alert as to what is going on in the financial industry. A recession may shake things up very fast, causing old industries to collapse (like the housing market) and fresh industries to be born (like the alternative energy market).

The data you gain may save you a lot of money and lead you to fresh opportunities. Make it part of your day-to-day routine to read a couple of articles every day and a couple of books each year.

Being prepared for opportunities is maybe the best technique you are able to have. The individuals who are out of debt and stay informed, may stumble upon a once in a lifetime opportunity.

I'm not a licensed financial advisor, so please confer with a licensed professional before making any investing or financial decision.

CHAPTER 7 – BEST LEGAL STRATEGIES TO KEEP BUSINESSES FROM CLOSING

Aside from the average people who lose their jobs whenever the economy is under the influence of economic recession, companies and businesses experience even more of the negative effects. The negative condition of the economy can affect these organizations in several ways that include slower demand, crashes within the stock market and increasing unemployment rates. These are all the usual effects of recession in the companies regardless of the industries they belong to.

The following are the strategies used by the companies throughout the period when the economy of a country is under recession:

Retention

The main priority of all types of businesses during the recession period is to retain their employees if possible and its culture as well as the values so that they can keep all their existing clients. Most of

Celebrate Recession with a Bottle of Champagne!

the companies and businesses around the world tend to provide their employees with a lower amount of compensation and even some offerings like free meals to lessen the higher cost of expenditures of the company for a while. This strategy will last until the companies and businesses know that economic recession still affects the countries where they are located.

On the other hand, there are some economists who believe that the turnover will oblige the companies to spend more than 100,000 dollars for every mid-level worker they have. This will be done if certain factors such as interviewing, recruiting, training, lost production and hiring are calculated. When it comes to the values of business, marketing and its image, it is necessary to keep the true identity of the business during the period of recession whenever it is possible. Aside from its help in keeping the high credibility and morale of the companies, this would also show the customers the strength of the company and that it is still capable of answering the needs of its customers despite the negative effects of the economy.

Pricing

Most of the businesses tend to drop quickly throughout the recession. It is necessary to maintain the costs of the products or services they offer on their neutral level while the short term cuts as well as the hasty deals of the business eventually cause a large rate of profit loss. The economists see that the substantial cost appears as a panic sign that the consumers would recognize. They will attempt to abuse the company and change suppliers and this will cause the business or company involved to lose more in terms of its share.

To prevent this situation, the economists argue that businesses should be confident and be aware of how far they will be able to compromise. When the companies work with new clients, they should recognize the opportunities and try to become accommodating to the clients as possible.

"Flanking" Products

The economists also suggest that the items with expensive values should keep their prices to protect their image and credibility as high quality products that cannot be provided at cheaper costs. Those consumers who really want these products will continue to buy them even if the prices remain the same.

To accommodate the clients who are no longer capable of buying expensive products, the companies and businesses should form a product line that the economists call "flanking products". These are the products that could satisfy the needs of the average customers with lower product quality and that are offered with no free service delivery but with reasonable costs.

By providing these products to answer the needs of other customers, the companies and businesses will be able to accommodate more customers who cannot afford high cost products. Likewise, there are some customers who prefer to buy everything they need in their daily living with no trade-ins. Therefore, companies will be able to get higher sales without changing the usual costs of the products they offer.

If you are a business owner, you know that you need to take some actions to save your company and make it survive throughout the economic recession period. These legal strategies will be the ultimate measures that can help your business in surviving and winning the race that will lead to riches. These strategies are used by those companies which are in good standing in the industry despite of the negative condition of the economy.

CHAPTER 8 – ACCEPT THE POSSIBILITY OF A MOVE

Your mortgage payment is probably your biggest monthly bill. Reduce your mortgage with one of the many options including downsizing, doubling up, and renting, refinancing or even foreclosing.

Assuming you can't sell your home... here are some ideas

If you purchased your home with 0% down and it's worth less than your real estate loan, then your most beneficial option is to just foreclose. You've nothing to lose but your credit – which will be repaired with time anyhow. But, if you've a significant sum of money in your home, then foreclosing is a much more difficult choice – and in this case you need to consider your long term financial outlook.

If you're likely to lose your job in the following few years, then you ought to think about foreclosure now instead of sometime in the future. There are lots of houses for rent and the cost of renting is really low because of the many houses that are not selling, so you'll find another place to live.

If you're planning to foreclose, call your lender after a couple of months of missing payments and ask for a nonrecourse foreclosure, which entails the bank accepting the house as full payment and provides up their right to try to get any more money from you in the time to come. (You should refer to a licensed pro before making any of these conclusions)

If you wait it out, all mortgage lenders are sooner or later going to be in very hard positions. Sooner or later your lender will be forced to do whatever they may to keep you from foreclosing, even if it means forgiving 50% of your loan worth.

Life isn't fair, and it's not going to be fair when the cat next to you gets his mortgage cut in half while you yielded full price. If your lender won't shift, then ask to refinance at a lower fixed rate. If your lender still won't shift, as most lenders are only talking terms with delinquent borrowers, try not paying your mortgage for a couple of months and then ask again. If the home is your primary residence, think about renting a room to a university student.

If there's a college in your area, just put up circulars on the college bulletin boards advertising your room for rent – accenting the many rewards of living in a house vs. a dormitory.

How about a college exchange student?

Telephone your local college and ask about their exchange student plan. College exchange students are students from other nations that visit the US by attending a US college. You are able to likewise try finding a niece or nephew in your family tree that would like to try living on their own.

This idea is particularly enticing if you live in a distant place from your niece or nephew for of the added adventure of traveling to a new place and experiencing new things. You are able to also market the advantages of living in a house to apartment renters, by placing flyers on apartments in your area. You are able to offer advantages like, a garage, a yard with a nearby park, an individual entry or allowing pets.

There are a lot of individuals in apartments that would love to enjoy some of the advantages of home owners. Find another family to live with you and partake in the costs of your home. This works great if you've a house that's naturally separated like a rambler with a finished basement as it gives each family the privacy they require.

The kids will likely love the idea of more kids to play with and if you're lucky one of your kids can sit for both families from time to time. This thought can likewise cut the chores in half as both families help to sustain the house.

To discover a great family to double up with, just ask around your acquaintances, family, church or other social groups that you're involved in. Leverage your home as office space to begin a home business. Utilize an extra room for your home office.

Your home business wouldn't have to use up all your spare time, just enough to help you pay your mortgage. I advise that you begin very small. The Net is among the best places to seek home businesses. You may try selling things on eBay.com or affiliate marketing or any number of things. You may likewise call a few local businesses and ask if there's anything you are able to help them with from your home office, like accounting or letter writing or dictation or anything else.

A small income from a home business may be just enough to keep you out front of your mortgage payments, and you are able to leverage the office space of your home to get it. A home business is likewise a good tax shelter.

ABOUT THE AUTHOR

Marc Foster is a business strategist. He is the head behind the campaign "Recession-Proof Businesses," which aims to enlighten business owners how to prepare for the next economic crunch and therefore avoid closing down unexpectedly.

Marc holds a degree in economics. He used to work for the stock market but took up consulting upon his retirement in 2006.

He is married with three children.

www.ingramcontent.com/pod-product-compliance
Lightning Source LLC
Chambersburg PA
CBHW070839220526
45466CB00002B/828